Paul the Author
Book 19

Written by G. Grafi
©2021

For Avihu and Liat;
You don't always choose your
family, but I gladly choose
you as friends who also
happen to be family.

A note to parents and teachers:
This is the nineteenth book in
the Rapid Reading series. Its
purpose is to practice the
diphthongs "au" and "aw".

Follow the guide and use the
tables on the next page to
practice the diphthongs "au"
and "aw" prior to reading the
book in order to facilitate the
reading process.

Sight words are high frequency
words that often repeat
themselves in many beginning
books. Sight words are
remembered rather than read.
It is recommended to practice
sight words as well.

Dr. G. Grafi

"au" and "aw" in this book.

Paul	August
author	launch
pause	saucer
laundry	auto
haul	autumn
faucet	applauded
exhausted	audio
because	taught
cause	

crawl	awe
yawn	saw
draw	squawked
drawings	claws
awful	scrawled
flawed	awesome
dawn	
lawn	
jaw	

Sight Words in this book.

before	one
chores	could
would	some
floor	ready
often	people
who	taught
were	other
was	

This is Paul. Paul is an author.

Before Paul can author a book,
he needs to pause to do chores.

Paul did his own laundry
and hauled it to its place.

Paul would crawl to clean
the floor and get up to clean
the faucet.

Often, Paul would pause
and yawn because he
was exhausted.

After resting, Paul would
haul himself to his desk.

Paul was an author who liked to draw his own drawings in his books.

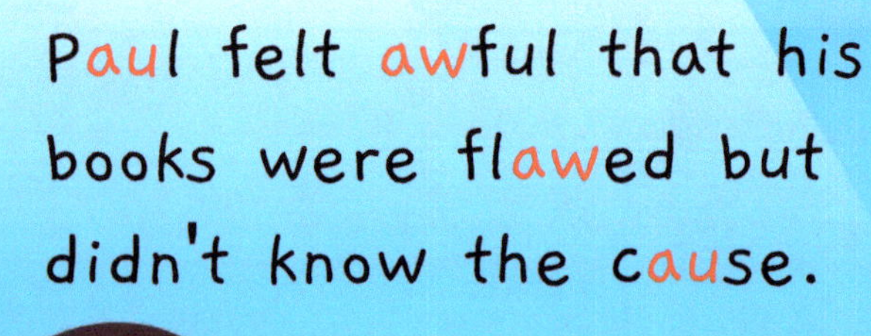

Paul felt awful that his books were flawed but didn't know the cause.

One dawn morn in August,
Paul was sitting on his lawn.

Paul could not launch a book because he paused his work.

He saw a flying saucer and his jaw dropped because he was in awe.

He launched the saucer and
saw that it was on auto pilot.

Paul reached a star and saw aliens with hawks as pets.

The hawks squawked and
had sharp claws.

Paul scrawled some notes
for his new book.

Paul came home in the autumn and was ready to author a new book.

Paul authored a new awesome book about the hawks.

BOOK SHOP

People applauded and got the audio book, too.

Paul's books were good, and he taught other authors, too.